A YEAR OF ZEN

A YEAR OF ZEN

A 52-WEEK GUIDED JOURNAL

BONNIE
MYOTAI
TREACE

ILLUSTRATIONS BY
VERÓNICA COLLIGNON

ROCKRIDGE
PRESS

Interior and Cover Designer: Brieanna Hattey Felschow
Art Producer: Hannah Dickerson
Editor: Vanessa Ta
Production Editor: Ruth Sakata Corley

Illustrations © Verónica Collignon, 2020

ISBN: Print 978-1-64739-717-3

R0

THIS JOURNAL BELONGS TO

_____

"This old plum tree is boundless.

It forms spring; it forms winter.

It arouses wind and wild rain. It is

the head of a patch-robed monk;

it is the eyeball of an ancient

Buddha. It becomes grass and trees;

it becomes pure fragrance.

Its whirling, miraculous

transformation has no limit."

—Master Dogen, priest
and teacher, founder of
the Soto School of Zen

INTRODUCTION

Zen will steal your tongue, and then ask that you speak. It will deliver you to the territory of utter intimacy, and make clear that whatever you say about it only moves you away from it. No one is immune from Zen's truth: we each and all suffer the demand that we express the inexpressible. We wake up in this demand every day, and seek sleep in the evening even as it presses on our heart. Think about it: your life is an astonishing improbability. Every single moment has a fresh face. And absolutely no one but the one reading this right now has what it takes to fully realize your precise possibilities. There is heavy responsibility to this, as well as the lightness of a feather, floating in the invisible wind that will bring the affair to perfect rest. Perhaps Meister Eckhart was right: "If the only prayer you ever say in your entire life is thank you, it will be enough."

In this journal comprised of daily writing exercises, you are invited to shape space, to create time. It will meet you on each day of the year, asking that you, as Zen always asks, "forget the self." And it will ask you to then take up the seeming contradiction of "When the self is forgotten, what is self-expression?" It cannot be escaped (short of intentional muteness, but that also speaks quite loudly), and it is not esoteric. Who hasn't so loved that all words failed? Or so grieved? The moment of memorial arrives, and the time for love songs. We enter language knowing it will fall short but is imperative.

That imperative is the practice taken up in this book. You are at the threshold, leaving all that was in place in the silence, now called to take a step. Make a mark. Create and reflect life, not knowing quite what it is or might become. In other words, read an assignment, and pick up your pen and write. Some days this will be straightforward, other days it may feel challenging, and you'll be unsure if you even understand what's being asked. Just write. Or draw when it is asked. Don't think about it too much.

I've taught Zen Journal retreats for many years. In most, the prompts would then be followed with 10 to 20 minutes of timed writing as Zen practice. I encourage you to have an additional blank journal and to pick perhaps one assignment each week and do a longer practice than the smaller spaces in this book allow. Why? The question begs the same question as "Why anything at all?" Why meditate? Why answer when someone calls? The quick and short daily notations help us to not overthink our writing; the longer ones let the mind and heart stretch into what's being considered. I hope you can trust that what's at play speaks directly to the impulse to live genuinely, with generosity and fierce clarity.

This book proposes a year dedicated to realizing that impulse: not just yearning or believing, but practicing, giving life to it. Each week the writing exercises will bring attention to seven areas: meditation, liturgy, work, body, study, art, and the world. Some areas will be easy for you to write about; others may feel more challenging. Pay attention to where you feel that particular push: it's indicating a ripe place to grow. For instance, Zen liturgy points to the intimacy between the self and all beings and things; this may seem unlike other rituals you might be more familiar with. Ritual may seem irrelevant, or have baggage for you. See what opens up as you let yourself explore. In the last exercise each week (World Practice), we'll check our moral and ethical pulses, turning attention to compassion, responsibility, and ways this great earth supports us. Each season will emphasize natural shifts in weather, social patterns (such as holidays), the changing dynamics of silence and light. You can start your writing at any week in the year. Each of the seasons are thirteen weeks (so, roughly: spring is March through May, summer is June through August, autumn is September through November, and winter is December through February). Sometimes a phrase or point will be used once, and then appear again slightly changed in another season. Here and there a Zen teacher will be briefly mentioned. If the taste of their teaching resonates on your tongue, please seek out their words, and let them nourish you.

We'll course through the mundane and the holy, the excruciatingly sad, and the fully wondrous. It will be a changing and sacred year. It always is, but this go-round we are creating it together. And that is everything.

Thank you for your attention, practice, and courage.

SPRING

In Zen, we talk of the "Vast Spring" that cracks a person open, shattering the edges that had seemed to confine the self, that had locked everything in separateness and pain. In the Vast Spring, every moment is verdant, full of unknown life. The stream unfreezes, and sings out the "eighty-four thousand hymns." The truth of spring is familiar, yet in our measureless long winter, we somehow forget what is real. We look at the frozen ground and deny that spring is there, hidden under three feet of snow. Still, there comes a primordial tapping: in the tree outside our kitchen sink, amid all the daily dramas we've defined ourself with, a bird's nest is visible. Listen! The chick is pecking from inside, the mother bird on the branch is pecking, too. Tender life will break free. In its small bones, the whole sky waiting. How will you practice spring?

> *"You can cut all the flowers, but you
> cannot keep Spring from coming."*
>
> –Pablo Neruda

PRESENT MOMENT: If you miss the moment, you miss your life. Take a moment to note this very moment: what do you see, hear, feel, notice most vividly?

....

....

....

....

....

....

GRATITUDE: If we spend our days complaining, our complaints become increasingly real. The opposite is also true: we can fill our lives with gratitude. Make a quick list of "Gratitudinals"—things you appreciate right now.

....

....

....

....

....

....

....

....

WHAT IS NECESSARY: Much of our work is "filler"—not really to the point. Consider your work, and reflect on how to stay engaged in the heart of the matter. Explore in a few sentences.

....

....

....

....

....

....

....

....

....

BREATHING IS GOOD: Amazingly, we can forget to just breathe. Have you caught yourself "holding your breath" in a tense situation, exactly when a breath would help you relax?

....

....

....

....

....

....

....

....

....

LISTENING: From winter's relative silence, spring arrives singing. What spring sounds did you hear today? Give words to the song of spring.

....

....

....

....

....

....

....

CREATIVE CALL: A Zen teacher asked to draw the spring breeze painted a butterfly, lilting over flowers. How would you show something invisible? Write or draw the scent of rain without naming it.

COMMUNITY: Even those we consider our opposites in terms of belief systems or values are usually kind to their pets and other loved ones. What other good qualities and concerns do you have in common with your "enemies"?

STOPPING: Find a comfortable position and sit still for five minutes. What makes you want to move? Is there space between a sensation and the decision to move away from it? Explore.

DEVELOPING RITUALS: In the mundane nothing is sacred; in the sacred nothing is mundane. What daily action (making a meal, brushing teeth) might you slow down and practice as a sacred activity?

ATTENTION: What is your most-used tool at work? For some it is a computer, others a shovel. Write it a short note of appreciation. Mention what you really like about it.

TAKING CARE OF THE BODY: Zen monks chant before shaving their head, "This is the way I show my gratitude." What ritual of grooming might be a way you could "show your gratitude" (not just be self-absorbed)?

"NOT TWO": Consider a public figure you don't like, and when you see them, chant to yourself, "Not two, not two." They and you are one. How is that true; how does it feel?

....

....

....

FEAR HAPPENS: Public speaking tops the list of people's fears, hold-ing them back. How does fear impact your creativity and leadership? List three ways.

....

....

....

....

....

....

....

....

....

....

....

SERVING AND BEING SERVED: Every day people are working on your behalf, even before the sun is up. Hospital workers, grocers, firemen, public servants, trash collectors. How can you express your appreciation?

....

....

....

....

....

....

....

....

....

BREATHING/BREATH: Every breath is an ineffable gift. Close your eyes and simply feel the breath arrive, fill your chest, and release. List a few words to describe your breath just now (Smooth? Deep? Blocked? Stuffy? Relaxing?).

....

....

....

....

....

....

....

JUST THE RIGHT AMOUNT: Arrange one particular bowl to use while you have a silent, appreciative meal. Sit quietly and eat: really taste your food, the textures, flavors, scents. In Zen this is "oryoki," just the right amount. Describe.

....

....

....

....

....

....

....

ONE THING AT A TIME: You can't get the whole project done right now. You can do the first thing. And then, the next thing. What is the first thing?

....

....

....

TENDER TOUCH, YOUR MUDRA: Meditate with your hands in the "cosmic mudra": active hand rests palm up in lap, other hand palm up on top of it, knuckles overlapping, thumbs barely touching. How is your life, like the mudra, a circle?

BEING A CURIOUS BEING: In the expert's mind, there is one possibility; in the beginner's mind, there are many! What don't you know about spiritual practice? What are you most curious to explore?

BLANK PAGES: Why are we terrified of the blank page? To shift from seeing a demand to seeing the immense, benevolent spaciousness requires letting go of self-proving. With nothing to lose, write a line!

....

....

....

....

....

....

....

....

....

....

....

....

HONESTY AND TRUTH: Honesty is a deeply private commitment. When you study your heart-mind, where do you struggle most with being honest with yourself? With others? (Note: heart and mind are regarded as one thing in Zen.)

....

....

....

....

....

....

....

....

MAKING TIME TO SIT: To make time for meditation, hunt for the "small animals" of time, the small mouse of a minute hiding here and there. Being a great hunter, now sit down and breathe. Reflect.

....

....

....

....

....

....

....

NATURAL ACTIVITY: Liturgy is not holy hocus-pocus. It expresses the common experience of a group in a ritual way. It's as natural as singing together at a ball game, finding one voice, celebrating what is shared. What are a few of the natural liturgies, like weddings or ballgames, that you've been part of?

....

....

....

....

....

....

PLANNING TAKES PLACE IN THE MOMENT: Dwelling in the moment doesn't mean we never plan what we need to do. We just need to not so lose ourselves in ideas about the future that we're checked out. How can you keep in touch with the present (Is that the tea kettle whistling?) while planning?

....

....

....

....

WILD THING: Don't confuse Zen practice with controlling the self. Your wildness is your perfection. What is wild about you? (That hair on your chin? Your crazy laugh? Tell!)

....

HOW A TREE GROWS: Tree rings show that some years are fat with growth, others very thin and challenging. Both fat and thin years combine to make an upright tree. Is this a fat, big-growth year for you? Or thin?

....

WHAT IS THE SELF IN SELF-EXPRESSION?: "To study the self is to forget the self," Zen Master Dogen said. If so, what is the self in self-expression? Don't explain . . . express!

GOLD DUST IN THE AIR: Beautiful blossoms, but the pollen makes you sneeze. List three things in your life that require holding space for both their beautiful/valuable side along with some real challenges.

POSTURE: Zazen asks that we sit in the "noble posture of the Buddha," upright with dignity and balance. How is this posture for you, regardless of being cross-legged, kneeling, or in a chair?

CREATING A SHIFT: Don't carry your attitude, or anything else, into the moment. Make a small bow, and consciously and deliberately let go, watching whatever thoughts you're holding on to change. Did your mind "unstick"?

OUR REAL WORK: We can have many different jobs in our lifetime, but have one "real work." What might that be for you?

EGGS IN THE GRASS: Mysterious eggs! Whether in a bird's nest or hidden by a holiday rabbit, eggs are pure potential. Might you also be a "good egg" in this sense? How so?

MYSTERY OF THE JOURNEY: Every year, monarch butterflies make a journey across several continents. Twice! How is your flight guided by the earth, wind, companionship of the like-minded?

WHO IS YOUR POET?: List some word wizards. If you don't have a list of poets or poems that shift your breath and help you see more directly, wondrously, is there some other muse gang (potters, painters, musicians, etc.) who do this for you?

NOT LYING: Little lies can seem harmless, and are sometimes necessary "social grease." But sometimes we know we've moved off center, and are just protecting a self-idea. Reflect.

SITTING COMFORTABLY: Gravity is your friend! Establish a meditation posture that puts you in a good relationship with it: not tilted, not wobbly. Reflect on this as a metaphor for daily life.

MAKING AN ALTAR: Earth, air, fire, water are represented on a Zen altar by a flower, incense, a candle, and a little bowl of water. This brings the whole earth to the table. Here we are halfway through spring: What is on your home altar? What are you forgetting to include?

SHOWING UP: Often we avoid what is difficult or confusing at work, only to find that all we needed to do was show up for it. Once we stop avoiding the problem, it is not actually such a big deal. Have you experienced this?

....

....

....

....

NOTHING BUT TADPOLES: Spring tadpoles remind us that we are nothing but change. Dance like a tadpole swims, like a froglet jumps. With one (squiggly!) line, draw that tadpole dance here:

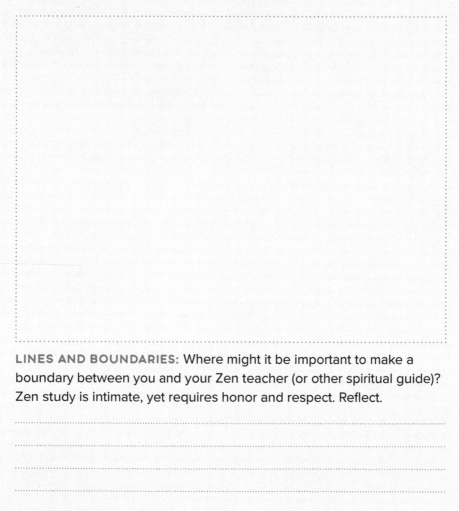

LINES AND BOUNDARIES: Where might it be important to make a boundary between you and your Zen teacher (or other spiritual guide)? Zen study is intimate, yet requires honor and respect. Reflect.

....

....

....

....

....

....

....

....

....

WHO IS YOUR PAINTER?: If you don't have paintings or painters who have shifted how you see, woken up your eyes, then list visual muses (your five-year-old's crayon drawings, that car ad, anything at all).

....

....

....

....

....

....

....

....

WHAT TO DO: Yasutani Roshi (1885–1973) taught that the keys to correct action are: Time, Place, Position, and Degree. What is appropriate now, not years ago. Where you live. Your role. How much or little serves. Reflect on these keys.

....

....

....

....

....

....

....

....

WANDERING MIND: Wander is what the mind does, and that's okay. To concentrate is also possible and good. Meditation involves both. Do you enjoy one more than the other? Why, do you think?

....
....
....
....
....
....
....

GASSHO: Bring left and right hands together, palm to palm. Two, realized and practiced as one: Zen calls this position "gassho." Gassho to people, places, situations. Where is this easiest? Hardest?

....
....
....
....
....
....
....

GIVING WITHOUT MEASURE: How can you be more generous at work? What gets in the way? List a few places you "measure your effort." How might you free yourself from holding back?

....
....
....
....
....
....

....
....
....

CHEAP CHI-KUNG: Stand with feet shoulder-length apart, arms loose at sides. Very slowly raise your arms over your head, making a circle, inhaling. Exhale as you circle hands back to your sides. Do this three times. Calmer?

....
....
....
....
....
....
....
....
....

THE TRAIL OF LOVE: Bliss, again! What about Zen, meditation, Buddhism makes you alive with curiosity? What can you do this week to explore those things a little further?

....
....
....
....
....
....
....
....

FLIGHT OF A BIRD: With a single line, draw the flight of a bird. Don't think too much, just do it.

THREE THINGS: Describe three things present in the best possible world you could create or leave for the next generations (or, three things that would be absent).

BEGINNER'S MIND: Settle into a seated posture to meditate and decide to stay for 10 minutes. Whenever a thought comes up about your meditation, meet it with "I don't really know." Then, let the thoughts go, and begin again, returning attention to your breathing.

BOWING A LITTLE: Whenever you come to a doorway or begin a new activity today, bring your hands momentarily into gassho, palm to palm, dropping whatever expectations you were carrying, and entering intimately. Tonight, write about how it was to slow down and bow.

START: It's amazing how long a project can take . . . if you never get started! Is there a project that you have been putting off? What one step can you make today to get it started?

SPRING PEEPERS: What if your heart was singing silently with simple happiness, as if being alive was a total turn-on?

INSPIRATION: We're adept at our cynicism, all the sad exhales, and may need help to remember to breathe in, to receive the love given over centuries. Who has inspired you? How so?

MOON IN A DEWDROP: Holograms have revealed that each small bit of a thing also contains the whole. A dewdrop has the ocean and the moon within it. So do you. How can you appreciate and celebrate this?

....

....

....

....

....

....

....

....

....

....

....

....

DEPTH OF THE DROP IS THE HEIGHT OF THE MOON: Is there a small act or statement you are aware of that changed the world in a big way? What is a small thing you might do to make the world better, clearer, kinder?

....

....

....

....

....

....

....

....

....

....

....

THE STILL POINT: What is the still point of the turning world? T. S. Eliot said it was neither "from nor toward." Reflect.

....

....

....

....

....

....

....

....

COURTSHIP DANCE: Consider the people you treasure. Like the birds and bees who dance and sing together during this season, how do you move in accord with these people?

....

....

....

....

....

....

....

....

LEAVING THE DRAMA BEHIND: Some of us have a habit of anger, others of depression. As you consider your work life, are either of these more of a habit for you?

....

....

....

....

....

....

....

....

STEP BY STEP: In Zen monasteries we transition from seated meditation to walking meditation very consciously. Practice being aware of the
sensations as you walk out of the room following your seated practice.
Does your mind become busier?

....

....

....

....

....

....

....

....

....

....

NO HEROES: Teachers fall from grace because they break their vows
or because we've held them in an idealized state. Has a spiritual
teacher, or anyone else you looked up to, ever disappointed you? Has
your understanding of that changed over time?

....

....

....

....

....

....

....

....

....

....

DRAW A LINE TRACING A TODDLER'S PATH: Conjure the image of a toddler toddling across a room, falling, recovering, laughing, crying. With a single line, draw that path:

I SEE YOU: All over the world sentient beings are suffering due to a myriad of reasons—natural disasters, diseases, social injustices. Let your mind and heart feel this as fully as you can. Consciously hold the hope that this suffering will be relieved, quietly repeating, "I see you." (This boundless warmheartedness is called Metta practice.) Reflect.

LOSING TRACK OF TIME: Have you ever meditated and had a minute feel like an hour? Or had 10 minutes pass as if it were just a few seconds? What changed in these experiences?

EMBODYING VS. BELIEVING: We can believe "we are all ultimately one," yet still act as if that were anything but true. What are some of the challenges for you in embodying that wisdom in compassionate action?

NEST BUILDING: It's a season of nest building. Have you built any "nests" (out of negative habits of mind) that you don't need? How might you build a different kind of nest to have shelter and rest when you do need it?

....

....

....

....

....

NO EDGE FOUND: Your body is permeable, bringing into itself what it needs to be healthy and alive, as well as sometimes what is unhealthy and dangerous. It's not always clear which is which. Are there ways you find this to be true?

....

....

....

....

....

....

....

BOOKS AND TEACHERS: To breathe in the room with a teacher is different than studying via books and media. Sometimes personality and style get in the way. Sometimes the living dialogue is essential. How have you experienced this?

....

....

....

....

....

....

PROCESS NOT GOAL: In art, as in life itself, focusing on the process rather than the goal is helpful. What is your experience with confusing the product with the practice? What helped kick you back into gear?

....
....
....
....
....
....
....
....
....
....
....

PRECEPTS: Zen has a list of precepts that outline how an awakened being lives their life with compassion, honesty, generosity, and moral wakefulness. Are they part of your life? What are three arenas where you encounter your ethical principles?

....
....
....
....
....
....
....
....
....
....
....
....

SILENCE: Silence is both external and internal. We are often quite starved for it, even as we may find it uncomfortable. What is your relationship to silence? How might it be deepened?

....

....

....

....

....

....

....

JOY: Some of the chants in Zen liturgy are pure sound and feeling, and don't have intellectual meaning. Along the lines of a great "yippee!" they celebrate the ground of being in this moment. Make a list of some of your joy liturgies—do you dance, sing, make music, make love?

....

....

....

....

....

....

....

FEEDING ONE ANOTHER: Heaven is where the beings feed one another with six-foot-long spoons across a huge table; hell is where beings starve because they try to feed themselves with those spoons at the same table and can't. How is your work likewise a mutual caregiving versus a solitary striving?

....

....

....

....

....

....

....

....

....

BEYOND THE RAISIN: One of the first mindfulness exercises people usually encounter is a very, very slow tasting of a raisin. Rather than gulping it down, the senses "get it" fully. Take one bite of your meal this way. What did you experience?

....

....

....

....

....

....

....

....

PLEASE EXCUSE ME: Some of us grow up as "the smart one." Some are on the other end of the continuum. When it's time to engage in learning or growth, where do you find yourself? What stories do you tell yourself? Are there particular excuses you frequently make based on your self-story?

....

....

....

....

....

....

....

BE A MAKER IN ONE BREATH: In one breath, draw a circle.

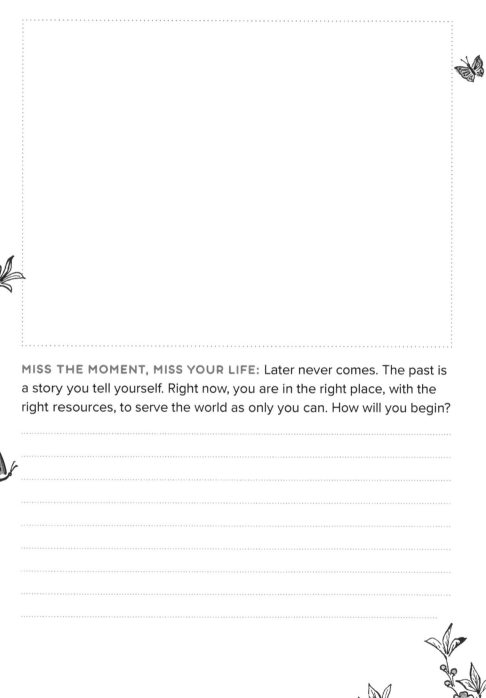

MISS THE MOMENT, MISS YOUR LIFE: Later never comes. The past is a story you tell yourself. Right now, you are in the right place, with the right resources, to serve the world as only you can. How will you begin?

WORKING WITH PAIN: In seated meditation, your foot might go to sleep. Your hip might be out of alignment a little. When you experience discomfort, try to simply experience it, not tell a dramatic story ("I'll never walk again," etc.). What have you learned from the passing nature of pain when you sit still?

GENUINE GESTURE: Zen liturgy asks that each gesture we make be honest. The teaching is "When you bow, just bow; when you chant, just chant." Have you been able to experience being this genuine? What can get in the way of that honesty?

FRONT OF THE ROOM: The Renewal of Vows ceremony in Zen asks that we vow to lead the people—not wait for someone else to do what is necessary, not defer. Sometimes we lead from the front of the room, sometimes from the back, invisibly. Where are you most comfortable?

FALLING BACK, THE TRUST EXERCISE: Ask someone to catch you as you fall backward into their arms. Do the same for them. Which position (catcher or caught) was easier for you? (You can also just imagine this.) Explore the implications.

WHEN EXPLAINING IS KILLING–ZENSPLAINING: Everyone has the inherent wisdom to awaken; each person is already, in a sense, a Buddha. Have you ever had someone "zensplain" (tell you about Zen as if you were an idiot); have you ever done this to someone else?

FOCUS: Give yourself 20 minutes and an apple. You're going to write about the apple. Its surface, juicy interior, round body, redness, life as a blossom, the hard fall to the ground or lightness of being plucked. Write, but keep coming back to the apple in front of you.

ANGER AND RESENTMENT: Injustice can create rage and profound resentment, both of which can be disabling and dangerous. It is imperative to find ways that address the deep pain and call to action injustice brings, and that enable a vital life. Write a few lines about your work with this issue.

TAKING CARE OF THE MIND: Some meditation halls prohibit crying; they're a little like pots about to boil over. Give yourself permission to have the full range of emotions as you sit. Are there things you think you shouldn't feel when meditating?

WHAT IF IT MATTERS?: Alone in a room, offer a stick of incense. Or make a full-to-the-ground bow. Not "to" anything, just to express the moment with utter sincerity. Does it matter what you do alone in a room?

BACK OF THE ROOM: Are you able to work invisibly, not drawing attention to yourself but making sure what is needed gets taken care of?

....

....

....

....

....

FINDING WHERE TENSION HIDES: Lie flat on your back, knees up on a low table or supported by pillows. Take five minutes to do a body scan, releasing tension gently, as if warm sand was simply flowing through you and into the ground. Where do you tend to hold tension?

....

....

....

....

....

....

....

THE LONG PATH: Do you find that you align or resonate with a spiritual or religious tradition? If you do, how so? If not, write a bit about not aligning with a tradition.

....

....

....

....

....

....

....

....

....

PATH OF A CLOUD: Imagine a blue sky. Imagine yourself noticing a wisp of cloud in the blue sky. There is a high wind moving the cloud from one horizon to another. In a single line, trace the path of your cloud.

THE GIVE AWAY: Spend an hour doing a bit of cleaning and organizing. As you do this, identify five things, large or small, that you could easily give away, donate, or need to throw away. Then follow up, and give them away!

SUMMER

Summer morning: everywhere you look there are dewdrops on the tips of innumerable blades of grass. Thousands of grasses, thousands of dewdrops. Have you awoken, or are you wandering in a dream? Zen speaks of "expressing a dream within a dream," acknowledging that we never quite rid ourselves of delusion and confusion, yet we can be present and fundamentally kind. There is so much bounty, so many tangled and twining vines, as well as so much lostness. Practice isn't about escaping any of it. It is about putting our feet on the ground, feeling the moist grass, knowing the wet stream of tears on a cheek, and not wandering off, looking for something better. "Here is the place; here the Way unfolds," Master Dogen wrote.

Summer, with its green canopy and sultry nights, asks that we not confuse enlightenment with distraction. Where there is a dream of intractable pain, Buddhas show up to be a salve to that suffering. They show up for you. They are not other than you. "Just as cages and snares are limitless, emancipation from them is limitless," Dogen also wrote. As you take up your summer pen, have trust in that freedom, and let yourself see and feel the causes and conditions whetting the grass tips in every direction.

ATTENTION MEANS ATTENTION: We kind of want spiritual life to be more complicated, but one of the greatest teachings in it is simply "Attention!" Where is giving your attention easy and natural for you? Where do you find yourself distracted on a regular basis?

....

....

....

....

....

....

....

....

LIGHTING THE CANDLE: Fire and light are represented on a Zen altar by a candle. Light a candle before you sit down to meditate, and summon your inner light, along with the mystery of fire. Reflect.

....

....

....

....

....

....

....

THE SCREW UP: Sometimes, we just screw up. We let people down; we don't get it done, whatever it is. Or we do the wrong thing. Take a moment and acknowledge a time or two when you have screwed up and then . . . let it go.

....

....

....

....

....

....

....

....

....

DON'T GET STUCK ON YOUR ZAFU: Make a vow before you stand up from your seated meditation that your practice will continue throughout your day. You'll keep beginning. Put that vow into simple words here:

....

....

....

....

....

....

....

....

SEVENTH GENERATION: Some of our teachers haven't been born yet. The generations that will follow ours are speaking to us. What do you hear them saying?

....

....

....

....

....

....

....

THE TEA MASTER: Find your cup, the one that fits your hands just right. As you make your tea or pour your coffee, let every sense be involved. Now, awakened by the drink and the awareness, write a few sentences about how to be a good and generous host.

....

....

....

....

....

....

....

....

....

....

SAVE THE DAY: Sometimes, we don't screw up. Instead, we are extraordinary. The impossible gets accomplished. Acknowledge a time or two when you experienced this and then . . . let it go.

....

....

....

....

....

....

....

....

....

....

....

THE POLICE STATE: Be cautious that you don't create a police state in your meditation. The rules about being still, focusing on your breath, etc., are meant to be life-giving. As you navigate the dynamic of developing discipline and yet not being internally mean, remember that deep intention. Tell your inner police to "Back off!"

....

....

....

....

....

....

....

....

....

....

NOTHING SPECIAL: Rituals can seem overly precious. Develop an antiprecious, nothing special attitude, willing to laugh at yourself if it gets overearnest and grim. Have you ever reacted to the "just-too-muchness" of liturgy or ceremony?

....

....

....

....

....

....

....

....

....

....

NON-DOING IS PART OF IT: Learn to take a two-minute vacation. Put down your baggage, let your shoulders relax, take a couple of good, deep breaths. How do you do "non-doing"?

WILD AND PRECIOUS LIFE: Mary Oliver ends her poem "Summer Day" by asking what you will do with this "one wild and precious life." What about your day today would be a response to her question?

WHAT IS THIS?: The name is not the thing . . . and neither is it otherwise. The word "mother" is not mother. Still, someone knowing our name can communicate love and respect. List the full names of five people you have loved, respected, or deeply appreciated.

ENFOLDED IN THE LEAF: There is a particular and tender darkness within the leaf before it unfolds. Put yourself into that darkness, and give it a name.

CLOSED EYES: Go sit for three minutes in a safe spot outside in nature with your eyes lightly closed. Write down the sounds you heard, in the sequence you heard them (just do your best).

KIND TO THE MIND: Practice speaking to yourself internally as you would to someone you deeply respected. What are some things it might be nice to say to yourself?

_____
_____
_____
_____
_____
_____
_____
_____

HONOR AND BLESS: There is a way in which when we honor something or someone, we are honored. When we bless, we are blessed. Who or what can you honor today? Where can you send your blessing?

_____
_____
_____
_____
_____
_____
_____

CROOKED PATH: Sometimes we need to go straight on a crooked path and take the next step, even if it isn't clear where we're going. What is a next step you need to take in your work?

_____
_____
_____

....
....
....
....
....

WALK, RUN, JUMP, DANCE: Surprise your body, waking it up with a different pace. Many of us get locked into just a few patterns of movement, and forget that we used to skip, jump, dance. How else can you move?

....
....
....
....
....
....
....
....
....
....

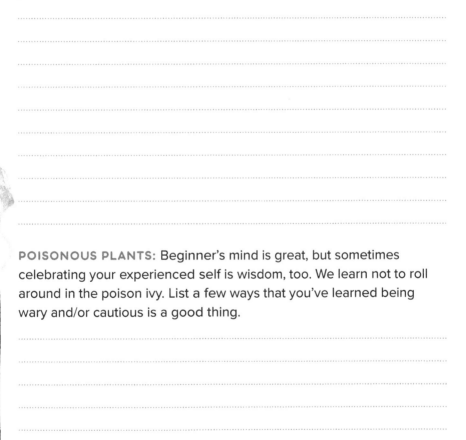

POISONOUS PLANTS: Beginner's mind is great, but sometimes celebrating your experienced self is wisdom, too. We learn not to roll around in the poison ivy. List a few ways that you've learned being wary and/or cautious is a good thing.

....
....
....
....
....

FULL COLOR: Play with language a bit; let yourself say what has never been said. To begin, give names to five new colors, like "milkapple pink," "rigorous trouble red," "poshnipple blue."

DEAR REPRESENTATIVE: Write a note to a political representative or public figure. Thank, encourage, guide: use "right speech," words that don't divide or elevate the speaker above the one addressed.

HAMMOCKS AND DOCKS: Sometimes the best meditation pillow is a hammock, a picnic blanket, a dock on the lake. Where have you meditated under the open sky?

....
....
....
....
....
....
....
....

MIDDLE OF THE BOWL: In Zen we offer burning sticks of incense sometimes to time a period of meditation, sometimes to recognize the passing-away-nature of all things. The stick is placed in the very middle of a bowl of ash (or rice), representing staying centered. Reflect gently on what has passed away in your life.

....
....
....
....
....
....
....

TOO HEAVY: What burden are you carrying at work that you might set down? Forever, or for just a while.

....
....
....

....

....

....

....

....

....

POSTURE OF AWAKENING: In Zazen we use the noble posture of awakening, sitting on the ground, unmoving, quiet. Try sitting for 10 minutes today with a promise not to move away from any sensation, and without narrating your experience. As you get up, thank the ground that supported you.

....

....

....

....

....

....

....

....

WHAT THEY SAID: Rewrite your favorite (Zen or other inspiring) quote in your own words.

....

....

....

....

....

....

ANIMAL ZEN: Bring an animal to mind. Close your eyes and imagine that when you open them, you'll see from the animal's point of view. What do you have in common? How is it adept in things you are not?

....
....
....
....
....
....
....
....
....
....
....
....

THOUGHT MATTERS: Karma (an action's tendency to continue) is created by what we do, say, and think. It creates our reality. What are a few thoughts that might lead toward the reality you'd like to live in?

....
....
....
....
....
....
....
....
....
....
....

MINDFULNESS: Close your eyes for a few moments and hear the sounds of your environment. Was there a sound that you hadn't been aware of?

....

....

....

....

....

....

....

FINDING FLOWERS: On a Zen altar, a flower is placed to the right of the Buddha image and represents the earth. Has a flower ever changed your mind or stopped you in your tracks?

....

....

....

....

....

....

....

....

SOMEONE WHO IS NOT BUSY: An old koan, teaching story, finds a teacher reminding his overly busy student, "You should know there is someone who is not busy." Can you find this not-busy-one, your inner stillness, in the midst of work?

....

....

....

....

....

....

....

....

OLD AGE, SICKNESS, AND DEATH: How does getting older teach you important things? What life lessons have you learned from sickness? Has encountering death ever brought life to your life?

....

....

....

....

....

....

....

....

I WILL NEVER GET THIS: To learn you have to let yourself be a beginner, to genuinely not know. Where is this easy for you? And where is it more difficult?

....

....

....

....

....

....

....

....

REVERENCE: Zen artists tend to be very reverential toward the tools of their trade (the tea utensils, the paint brush). Describe your pen, brush, musical instrument, etc., with the deep, precise attention that reflects that reverence.

PICK UP AFTER SOMEONE; SAY NOTHING: Just do it! What's it like to do something just because it needs to be done?

SLOTH AND TORPOR, TOO: Sometimes, we're just a mess. We want a nap and for someone else to take care of it all. And sometimes, we get lost and stuck in being sloppy. How do you awaken your caretaking mind?

....

....

....

....

....

....

....

WHEN IT FEELS SILLY: Buddhists do all sorts of silly liturgy: chanting or walking extraordinarily slowly, bowing to an incense stick, shaving off all our hair! What changes a silly action into something that expresses care, attention, and compassion?

....

....

....

....

....

....

PUT DOWN THE PHONE: Turn off your phone for a little while. And the computer. Track your mind: did you get agitated, feel more peaceful, or what?

....

....

....

....

THIS PAIN IS REAL: Though we can make pain much worse when we build a drama around it, there's no denying the bricks that fall on our heads on occasion. How has physical or emotional pain played a part in your spiritual life?

I WANT A DIFFERENT KOAN: For Zen students, as for all human beings, the "spiritual grass" frequently looks greener on somebody else's pillow. We want a different koan (challenge to our reality)! Reflect.

EPIPHANIES: List five of the great moments, shifts, or epiphanies in consciousness, wonders, awakenings, or fabulosities of your life.

THE BOOK THAT NEEDS TO BE WRITTEN: Pretend you are given the gifts and time to write a book that will make a huge, positive impact. What is its title?

RADICAL PRIVACY: Meditation gives you a doorway into a radically private space: your heart-mind. Are you comfortable there? Do you crave or avoid it? Or something else?

....

....

....

....

....

....

....

....

I TAKE IT BLACK: Think of the everyday liturgy of serving and receiving a cup of coffee or tea. Have you ever had your day changed by a kind look, an authentic thank-you, or a routine that felt genuine?

....

....

....

....

....

....

....

....

WASH YOUR BOWL: The Zen master asked a new student, "Have you eaten?" The student said, "Yes, I have." The master said, "Go wash your bowl." When we're full of the last meal, the prior insight, we have no room for what arrives. Any chance you, too, need to "wash your bowl"?

....

....

....

VULNERABLE ALWAYS: A mountain climber returns from a huge adventure and falls on a dime-size piece of ice on her front step; she lives the remainder of her life in a wheelchair. How does vulnerability impact your willingness toward adventure?

IF NOT ME, WHO; IF NOT NOW, WHEN?: There's no one else and no other time to take care of your spiritual life. What needs taking care of today?

NOTE: Write a note to yourself five years from now. What do you want to be sure to remember?

LEAD THE PEOPLE: Thank a leader, someone who left the world a more compassionate place. Be specific about what you appreciate.

SO MUCH ATTITUDE!: Our meditation posture reflects our attitude: down in the dumps (slump!); feeling proud (chin juts out!). Try tucking your chin in a bit, taking a moment to relax your jaw and release any tension at the top of your spine. As you "get your head on straight," does your inner attitude shift?

....

....

....

....

....

....

....

CHANTING: Pick a couple of words to chant to yourself today, "I am" or "Not two," for example. Like a song lyric, let it repeat, then let it go. Reflect.

....

....

....

....

....

....

....

LEAVE NO TRACE: When we leave one space for another, a good practice is to leave no trace. In other words, clean up after yourself. Is this easy for you? Or difficult?

....

....

....

....

ALTERNATE NOSTRIL BREATHING: Sit quietly, close your eyes, and place the pointer and middle fingers of your right hand on your "third eye." Press your right nostril gently closed with your right thumb and inhale. Then release it and close your left nostril using your fourth finger, and exhale out your right nostril. Continue for several breaths, inhaling into one nostril and then out the other. Most people are calmer after several cycles of this. Are you?

BUDDHISM IS BIG: List a few things you'd like to know, explore, study, or hear about in Zen, Buddhism, or other spiritual practices.

DRAW A GREEN LEAF. DO NOT USE GREEN: Just do it! How do you indicate summer, green, verdancy without coloring the leaf green?

AT YOUR SERVICE: Today, and several days this week, be a servant of the world. Pick up trash, write an editorial, bake someone a cake— anything. What way(s) did you find to serve this week? What kinds of service make you feel particularly well-used?

RETURN TO ONE: Settle into a comfortable seated position, and for five minutes practice linking your breathing with counting to ten. Inhale, "one" . . . exhale, "two" . . . etc. When you reach ten, begin again at one. Did the counting help you stay focused?

....

....

....

....

....

....

....

NO MAGIC: Ceremonies aren't magic; they can, however, deepen and/or change how we see and embody ourselves and our relationships. Has this ever happened to you?

....

....

....

....

....

....

....

WHO'S IN THE KITCHEN?: Reflect on who transports your ingredients, cooks your meals, cleans up, takes out the trash, carries it away. In Zen we call this the 72 labors (a way of saying "so many!") that feed us. Who comes to mind for you?

....

....

....

....

....

....

....

....

CATCHING YOURSELF SHOWING OFF: Zoom and FaceTime are ways to notice the age-old desire to look good and maybe show off a little. Do you find yourself setting the stage and primping for social media? Or can you meet it just as you are in any moment?

....

....

....

....

....

....

....

....

IS IT YOU OR ME?: There are times when it's hard to tell if a teacher or guide is operating in terms of their own needs or guiding truly. What helps you be clear in this? What hinders?

....

....

....

....

....

....

....

....

....

ONE BREATH POEM: Write a few words (do it in a breath or two so you don't overthink!) that are summer itself.

....

....

....

....

....

....

....

....

....

....

REDUCE WASTE: What are some simple ways you might reduce your trash creation?

....

....

....

....

....

....

....

....

....

....

....

....

....

....

NOT COUNTING BREATHS: You've tried counting your breaths in meditation. Now, focus on your breath without counting. Was that harder or easier?

CHOPSTICKS AND SPOONS: The utensil we use can change how we relate to the life that is our food. Reflect on stabbing things with a fork versus lifting consciously with a spoon or chopsticks.

FIND YOUR VOICE: Write about a time at work when you needed to say something in a forthright way and did so.

....

....

....

....

....

....

....

....

....

WASH YOUR HANDS: In this age when we've learned how important it is to wash our hands, what might you do to experience this as pleasurable, wondrous, something you're grateful for?

....

....

....

....

....

....

....

....

FLYING LESSONS: Mother birds convince their young to step out into air when that seems impossible. Is there a time you moved forward when you didn't know how but did it anyway?

....

....

....

FIND YOUR MUSIC: What music makes you feel more alive? Have you noticed it change over time?

SING/CHANT WITH OTHERS: Reflect on a time when you sang, danced, or chanted with others. What is it like to find that greater expression made out of many creating together?

CRAZY LOUD BRAIN: Part of deepening into meditation is acknowledging the thoughts that arise. Write for a minute or two here with your stream of consciousness, just letting the pen move. If you don't know what to write, write, "I don't know what to write."

....

....

....

....

....

....

....

....

BUDDHA'S ROBE, YOUR BLUE JEANS: After morning meditation, Buddhists do a chant that identifies the Buddha's robes as the clothes they'll wear for the day. They dress not for success but for awakening. How do you feel about that?

....

....

....

....

....

....

....

LIGHTNING BUG TALK: Lightning bugs talk to each other with light. How can you talk with your coworkers without using words?

....

....

....

....
....
....
....
....
....

FEEL THE CUP: We can behold by holding. Hold your favorite or familiar coffee cup and just take it in silently. Describe.

....
....
....
....
....
....
....
....

NOT SURE WHAT THE TOPIC IS: In Zen, all the study with a teacher deals with one topic: Who are you? The teacher will use whatever is at hand to point back to that question. What has brought you to wonder about your self-nature recently?

....
....
....
....
....
....
....

HOW MANY SOUNDS?: Using a couple of found objects, create rhythm for two minutes. (Yes, bang on that pot!) What did that feel like?

....

....

....

....

....

....

....

....

....

....

MEET YOUR NEIGHBORS: Who are your neighbors? Are there ways you could be more there for one another? Who in your vicinity is aged/disabled/might sometimes need assistance or cheering up?

....

....

....

....

....

....

....

....

....

....

....

(WEEK 25)

BITE-SIZE PEACE: Take one breath in and let it go, all the way from your belly out to the end of the earth. Take a bite-size peace break several times today. Did it help a little?

72 LABORS BROUGHT US THE FOOD: It's not just the cooks and farmers—who else, in perhaps more subtle ways, contributes to bring you sustenance physically, emotionally, and spiritually?

YOU HAVE NO IDEA: Sometimes, there is nothing but working with mystery. Have you had times in your job, or work on behalf of others, where nothing felt clear? Then what happened?

SUMMER   75

....

....

....

....

....

....

....

ICE CREAM IN THE SUN: Some of us love a mess, others avoid it at all costs. And yet, being physical is unavoidably messy. Recount a memory of surviving the messiness.

....

....

....

....

....

....

....

....

....

NEW THOUGHTS: What did you like and dislike about a book, article, essay, or poem that you've read recently?

....

....

....

....

....

....

....

DRAW A LINE: Trace the sound of yourself breathing.

OTHER PLACES: Write down as many countries as you can in 60 seconds. Are there some countries and cultures that feel more "other" than the rest? Reflect on why and how or why not.

LOST IN SPACE: Meditation is not really a 1-2-3 process, though it is sometimes taught that way. In fact, we have to let ourselves be a little lost in order to find our true path and find the way we alone need to go. Reflect a bit on letting go of direction.

....

....

....

....

....

....

....

TEMPLE KITCHEN: In a Zen monastery, the kitchen is regarded as another part of the meditation hall. It is a place of sacred activity, where reverence for life is taken seriously. Can you find the temple in your kitchen?

....

....

....

....

....

....

SNAKES AND SNAKEBITES: One way to avoid stepping on a summer snake is to always step up onto a log in the path, not over it where the snake may be unseen in the shadows. How can you "step on the log" in your workplace, so you don't accidently rile a sleeping snake?

....

....

....

....

....

....

....

....

FLOAT: There are times when not trying so hard, but rather floating as if on the warm waters of a lake, is helpful. It is not time to *do*, but more of a time to simply *be*. Have you noticed this?

....

....

....

....

....

....

....

....

THE END IS NEAR: If there were only a few weeks left of your life, and you were full of energy, what would you need or want most to do?

....

....

....

....

....

....

....

....

....

WHISTLE THE FEELING OF BEING WITH A FRIEND: Or hum, or sing. But make a sound that expresses that feeling. What was that like?

....

....

....

....

....

....

....

....

....

....

....

....

COMPASSION: What is the kindest thing you remember witnessing or becoming aware of?

....

....

....

....

....

....

....

....

....

....

....

....

....

AUTUMN

The mind of autumn is aware of losing things. What had been so vitally unfurling throughout summer's heat goes the way of spent leaves. It is a time when we wonder whether things exist only to be lost, and in that, to become more precious, regarded in memory in ways even deeper than in presence. The monochrome green of summer explodes into hillsides of amber, gold, apples, and pumpkins. As the flaming, warm days depart, evening fires are lit, sweaters are knitted. We know we cannot hold on. We know winter is around the bend. There is nothing but a profound vulnerability, and yet every sense claims a kind of glory.

Engage the overwhelming sensuality of fall: your writing will make squash soups and pies whose scent may heal broken hearts. To write in sync with autumn is to be harvesting and harvested, the worker and the crop. The wind will move the leaves toward compost, setting them free to sail home to soil. There is no mistake, yet grief is real and undeniable. The most fortunate will reflect and draw together family and loved ones, celebrating connections and gathering strength for the cold days ahead. Study the sky and ground, letting the earth body tell you the truth. These are the weeks to let your words be touched with the pathos that gives thanksgiving its real heart.

WHEN YOU'VE LOST IT: There are times meditation will feel very centered, deep, even beautiful. And then we'll lose it, and find that our mind has become busy or rageful or petty. This is just being human, but it can be a hard ride. Reflect.

....

....

....

....

....

....

....

HARVEST: There are Buddhist practices where first you appreciate your loved ones, then those simply familiar, then strangers, and finally those who've been a pain. Write a thank-you to someone in one of these four categories for being part of your life and growth. Harvest the sweet and the bitter nourishment.

....

....

....

....

....

....

FAILING IS NO FUN: Consider what makes failing in certain areas of our work feel particularly significant. Are there areas of endeavor in which it is harder or easier for you to sometimes fail?

....

....

....

LIFE IS A MARTIAL ART: The martial arts teach that when facing an opponent, if you can, run. If you can't run, do the least amount of harm in the engagement. What would help you have the courage to back down from a fight?

ANIMAL ZEN: Have animals helped you be a better person? How? Who were they?

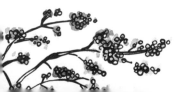

BE THUNDER: Without using your hands, show what lightning and thunder feel like. Now write a line about the silence that follows the storm.

TERRA: What kind of terrain is most comfortable for you? Most beloved or awe-inspiring? Least interesting?

WITH SNIFFLES: In a serious Zen meditation hall, you don't even wipe your nose. You just let it be, and keep meditating until the bell rings. How might stillness help when you're feeling a little under the weather?

THE FUTURE HAS A BIRTHDAY: It starts now. The future always seeds itself in now. Fill yourself with all the best wishes you'd have for a new-born, and make a birthday wish for the future.

CREATING GOOD TROUBLE . . . OR NOT: Have you ever had to make good trouble at work? To stand up for someone being mistreated? Stand in a picket line? Speak out against unfair treatment?

THE MIRACLE OF ALIVENESS: With unearned gifts left and right, we have this day! It will never be requited, but it can be celebrated. What are a few ways you might celebrate the miracle of aliveness today?

REAL TALK: It is inestimably helpful to have someone whom which you can delve into and explore your values and life and death decisions. Is there someone you can do this with when you need to? (If not living and present, is there someone you can call to mind for this purpose?)

LOTUS IN THE FIRE: The fires and muck of the swamp make the lotus bloom, feeding it what it needs to be itself, and offer beauty. Draw a quick sketch of a lotus in the fire or something that likewise expresses trust in your situation and life's natural unfolding.

END NOTE: Zen monks would carry just enough money in their pack for burial expenses, a teaching in taking responsibility. Are your final affairs organized? Communicated? If not, how can you move this forward and not leave this hard thing to others?

WHEN YOU HAVEN'T BEEN SITTING: It's been ages. And the longer you're away from sitting, the harder it feels to start again. *Everybody* goes through this, whether it's with meditation or physical exercise. The big secret? Difficult is okay. Just begin. Reflect.

....
....
....
....
....
....
....
....

GOOD DOGS DIE: Your heart breaks, you dig a hole, there are no sufficient words. Write a couple of lines about loss and love. Have you ever had to work to love again after a loss?

....
....
....
....
....
....
....
....

SOCIAL MEDIA MALAISE: This generation has more access to information and entertainment than any before. We're adept at jumping down the rabbit hole of endless distractions. The first step is to acknowledge the challenge. Where are you with this?

....
....
....

WITHOUT BREAKING A TWIG: In our preoccupation with where we're headed, we miss the steps. Practice walking, in the woods if you can, making as little noise as possible. What do you see when you put eyes in your feet and walk with the whole body and mind?

JUST FOR YOU: What is one thing that someone has said or written that seemed aimed directly at your heart?

THE WAY LEAVES FALL: Imagine five new names for the way leaves fall. Just play. Fill your inner vision with falling leaves and make up names for it, such as "caramel-turvy," "ambiguous-flitty," and "floppity."

CHEER UP A CRYING CHILD: Children don't calm down by being told to "calm down" (actually, no one does!). How do you delight or distract a child into laughter? Imagine this is a magic power you indeed have.

BEING LOVE: How do we "become" or "be love" itself? By loving. Find the wispy cloud of love, or its cousin the huge hurricane of love, and let it touch you (or bowl you over). Are there words?

....

....

....

....

....

....

....

....

HOW TO LET GO: The Zen teacher hands you a stick. "Let go," she says. You sit there, holding the stick in front of you, not sure what to do. She takes the stick, and says, "Like this." The stick falls to the ground as you both laugh. What is "the stick" in your life?

....

....

....

....

....

....

....

BUT THE WORLD IS ENDING: Nothing seems like enough or completely on point when civilization looks like it may be ending. It's easy to stagnate at work and feel overwhelmed. Even when things seem quite bad, however, certain people find ways to be kind, creative, and loving. Reflect.

....

....

....

....

....

....

....

....

MOON HOWL: There's nothing like a good howl. The body needs to be given over utterly to the immeasurable (sometimes drawn out by beauty, sometimes by sorrow). When do you need to howl into the great dark sky, the silent white moon?

....

....

....

....

....

....

....

RENGETSU THE UNSTOPPABLE: Buddhist nun Rengetsu (1791–1875) faced more heartbreak than should be humanly bearable (deaths of her children, loss of religious sanctuary, betrayal and death of spouses, and more), yet she would go on to be one of Japan's greatest artists, mystics, poets, and teachers. Write her a short note here.

....

....

....

....

....

....

DRAW THE CAPITAL LETTER A: Draw the letter "A" as beautifully as you can. Let it stand for the beginning of a new alphabet, a renewed language.

GOOD PEOPLE: Many or most people aspire to be their understanding of a good person. Reflect on times where you've come to understand that what first struck you as someone being controlling or lax was them doing their best to be good but by a different definition than you hold.

DON'T MEDITATE: Meditation may not be what is called for. You have a fever. You're mortally depressed. You've been up all night. Sometimes it's more appropriate to rest or get professional help. Do you find yourself being too demanding of yourself at times, rather than simply and steadfastly developing your discipline and commitment?

WRITE YOUR MEMORIAL VERSE: Write a short poem that helps those who will hear it after you have died.

GENDER ATTENTION: How has your gender impacted your work life? List five small ways or one big.

....

....

....

....

....

....

ACCESS: Many public places, including zendos, are still not set up using universal design that accommodates people with disabilities. Has this been part of your experience?

....

....

....

....

....

....

....

....

....

....

SCREENS: Have your reading habits changed since most people now read mostly from screens? How do you feel about this? Do you miss the softness of paper? What else comes to mind?

....

....

....

....

....

....

....

....

YOU'VE GOT MAIL: Send yourself an appreciative, funny email as if you were your own best friend.

FIERCE LOVE: Being a person of Zen (someone who practices their life) doesn't mean being passive or having no passion. It in fact involves being immensely, intimately interconnected with "all sentient beings in the 10 directions." Their suffering is yours; and you are charged to act with compassion and creativity. Still, you have the capacity to not get lost in anger and reactivity. Reflect.

WISDOM: In the Zen tradition, there's more to meditation than stress relief. It is also about waking up to one's true, unbounded nature, and living one's life from that reality. Some students have a spiritual hunger for wisdom; others trust it is expressed constantly and there is nothing to seek. How about you?

....
....
....
....
....
....
....

AUTUMN VERSE: Write a short poem of three or four lines expressing your readiness to release your "dead leaves" and trust in the new life this will free you to create.

....
....
....
....
....
....
....

GETTING THERE: Whether it's just walking to the desk in your home office or taking several trains and taxis, buses, or bike rides, is your transition into work mind conscious? Write a brief dedication to give attention to this transition.

....
....
....

EVERYBODY SLUMPS: Gravity, or our mood, wins some days, and we find we're just kind of slumped over with it all. The secret to getting upright? Noticing the slump. How can you get in a better relationship with gravity? With your mood and mind?

STUDENT MIND: No one is essentially better than you, nor worse than you. Yet teachers sometimes teach—wittingly or unwittingly—as if coming from a lofty place, and we feel lesser than. What are your challenges to developing student mind, yet staying aware of your basic perfection?

SIMPLICITY: Keeping it simple, draw a straight line.

TIGHT AND LOOSE: Some cultures are "tight" and really like things to happen on time and in accord with the agreed-upon rules. Others are more "loose" and give leeway in terms of being late and breaking rules. Where do you fall?

COUCH POTATO: We all sit—whether it's watching TV from the couch or cross-legged on a meditation pillow. It's helpful to set up a particular place you'll sit for meditation. Where do you meditate?

....
....
....
....
....
....
....
....

THESE WORDS HAVE NO MEANING: Some Zen chants have no translation and are just pure sounds (like "yippee" or "ouch" are pure sounds needing no translation to be understood); they function more like instrumental music than intellectual teaching. Reflect.

....
....
....
....
....
....
....
....

NO VOTE: There won't be a group vote on whether we've led a good life or done good work. The metrics can change after we die, with what was once acceptable or good becoming judged by new factors. How do you motivate yourself to do your best?

....
....
....

....
....
....
....
....

NOT A SOLDIER'S ATTENTION: The meditative posture is upright, but relaxed. The mind state is awake, but not tense. For many, it can be a revolution to relax and not just fall asleep. How is it for you?

....
....
....
....
....
....
....

NO WORD SLAVES: In an apparent paradox, Zen literature places great attention on there being no dependence on words and letters. How can you make what you study really your own?

....
....
....
....
....
....
....

DARING: Are there ways you need to "fly free from the tree" in your life, your art, your relationships?

....
....
....
....
....
....
....
....
....
....
....

STOP THE PROGRAM?: Every person is conditioned from birth, programmed by parents, peers, teachers, culture. Do you think it's possible to break free from this robotic existence?

....
....
....
....
....
....
....
....
....
....
....

STARTING AGAIN, AGAIN: We reach a refined place. A good state of mind. We begin to believe we've reached enlightenment. And then: we treat someone poorly. Does this mean that practice has done nothing?

PILGRIMAGE: Consider an intentional journey, one in the direction of the mountaintop, the place where it is clear how all the parts of the terrain fit together. Now come down off the mountain into the marketplace. What are the challenges?

WRITER'S BLOCK: If we hold a quiet belief that if we were seen clearly we'd be rejected, our creativity will stagnate. What if all and every part of you was accepted?

BREATHING WITH YOUR TOES: Sit in a chair. Imagine your breath coming in your big toes, then being exhaled. Move to the next toe, and continue with full cycles of the breath until you reach your smallest toe. (This is a great practice for dental procedures, by the way.) Reflect.

REPETITION: There are scales in spiritual practice, just like in music, things you go over and over, even after many years. Have you experienced doing the same thing and found something brand new?

MAKE YOUR INK: The Zen sumi-e painter uses the time mixing the black ink they paint with as a meditation. They slowly rub the ink stick in the small tray of water, preparing both ink and mind. Do you have a meditative way to enter art practice?

WATER RETURNS TO THE OCEAN: Do you know where your tap water originates? Knowing a bit about your watershed is a way to understand how connected many life systems are. What is your relationship and responsibility to water?

NOT-KNOWING: A Zen student says to their teacher, "I've realized not-knowing!" The teacher replies, "How do you know?" Have you experienced turning intimate life into things, descriptions, in such a way that you lose track of true intimacy?

....

....

....

....

....

....

....

KEEPING RITUAL SIMPLE: "When you bow, just bow," the Zen saying goes. In other words, don't get lost in the words and ideas: just practice. To bow is to express nonseparation. Where might it be easy for you to bow? Where difficult?

....

....

....

....

....

....

WHEN ALL ELSE FAILS, MAKE PIE: Sometimes we turn work into a grim and aggressive place. What are a few ways you might take the ingredients of your life and bring to the table a little more joy, pleasure (pie?), fun, and creativity?

....

....

....

....
....
....

HEAD SHAVING AND HAIR WASHING: When a Zen student takes monastic vows to become a monk or nun, they shave off their hair. Every time they shave, they dedicate the letting go of vanity (and hair) as a way of expressing gratitude. Try taking an act of grooming, like hair washing, and shifting it from preening to a time of dedicating your day to compassion. Reflect.

....
....
....
....
....
....
....
....

BODHIDHARMA: Bodhidharma (483–540), legendary founder of Zen in China, said Zen is "Pointing directly at the human mind, seeing its nature, and becoming Buddha." In other words: this is not about understanding Buddhism, but understanding yourself. How do you take this up directly and deeply?

....
....
....
....
....
....
....

ZEN CIRCLE: Draw a circle, beginning at the bottom, and not quite closing it as you come around. Leave a little space for the viewer to complete it in their mind. Where else in your life might you leave that small space that lets others in?

....

....

....

....

....

....

....

....

....

WOMEN LEADING: In Zen history, like much of world history, women seldom received the full support in their spiritual lives that men did. Still, both as monastics and lay women, they persevered and provided uncommon leadership and inspiration. What do women bring to the picture that is needed?

....

....

....

....

....

....

....

....

....

....

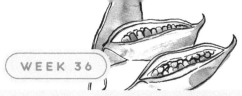

JUST WEATHER: As you meditate, the thoughts that flow through awareness become less of a big deal than awareness itself. Awareness is like the sky that weather happens in. Have you been able to shift focus from the passing weather to that sky?

BETWEEN BELLS: We ring a lot of bells in Zen. Three bells begin a period of meditation. Two bells signal it's time to stand up. The space between the sound of the bells is important. How so?

EXCELLENCE: The autumn leaves scatter and pile up randomly. Our efforts can seem likewise to land differently than we intended or imagined. Does it matter, then, if you commit to excellence in your work?

HAKUIN'S MELTING EGG: Master Hakuin (1686–1789) taught that to relax, imagine a duck egg-size lump of butter suddenly on your head. As it melts, it fills your head and entire body with an exquisite warmth, until you rest waist-deep in a comforting bath of fragrant and medicinal herbs. Has visualization ever helped you?

MAHAPRAJNAPATI: Born in 600 BCE, Mahaprajnapati was the Buddha's aunt and wanted to study with him. He refused her, but she followed anyway, walking until her feet bled. Thousands of women joined her. By persisting, she opened the door for all women, and was ordained. Who has opened doors for you?

EMPTY THE CUP: You can't receive that delicious cup of apple cider if your cup is already full. You can't receive teaching, or grow, if you are already convinced there is nothing to receive. How do you empty your cup?

....

....

....

....

....

....

....

....

....

....

GATHER THE WORLD: Make a list of who you'd invite to a Gratitude Dinner. Who, from all your experience, from all of history, from near and far, living and dead, would it be nice to serve a good meal to, have warm conversation with, say the thank-you that doesn't quite fit into words?

....

....

....

....

....

....

....

....

....

....

PRESS DELETE: When we have a negative interaction with someone, we sometimes use meditation to simply replay it over and over, setting ourselves up with a script of high drama. What if you just pressed Delete?

....

....

....

....

....

....

....

THE BUDDHA'S BOWL: Zen students use oryoki bowls to receive meals meditatively. Oryoki means "just the right amount." In what areas of your life is it most challenging for you to practice receiving what you need gratefully, without falling into excess?

....

....

....

....

....

....

....

CLEAN OFF YOUR DESK: Before you stop work at the end of the day, clean up your work space so that when you arrive the next day, it is spare and supports your fresh attention. How is this for you?

....

....

....

....
....
....
....
....

AUTUMN IS NAP WEATHER: What gets in the way of your resting deeply for a sufficient amount of time? List three things you can do to support yourself in the fine art of being well-rested.

....
....
....
....
....
....
....

DOGEN ZENJI: When Zen Master Dogen (1200–1253) ran his community of monks, he made every aspect of the day a spiritual practice—cooking, cleaning, being an administrator, even going to the bathroom, all became places to wake up. What one everyday activity could you begin to make a spiritual practice?

....
....
....
....
....
....
....

BARRIERS: Have you ever experienced a barrier becoming a gate? What if everything that seemed to stop you from being creative had within it exactly the key to your next creative act? What if, for instance, the thought "I have no time" became your inspiration for a notebook of thirty-second haiku or drawings?

....
....
....
....
....
....
....
....
....
....

CIVILIZATION REDUX: Imagine compassion was central to all the decision-making in our civilization. What do we most need to work on that presently blocks that from happening? What are a few ways you can work on this?

....
....
....
....
....
....
....
....
....
....

THIS IS ABSURD: An absurd statement: the child says, "The dinosaur ate my homework." What is an absurd excuse for not meditating? Or, an absurd reason *to* meditate?

....
....
....
....
....
....
....
....

SUNDOWN THRESHOLD: Catch yourself at sundown, light fading from the sky. What does the arrival of night trigger or bring up for you?

....
....
....
....
....
....
....
....

FIRE IN THE BELLY: What work might ignite a fire in your belly, a powerful sense of dedication? Are you presently engaged with this work?

....
....
....
....

FORGIVING THE BODY: This miraculous physical body . . . yet we so often are a little angry at it. It trips, sickens, gets flabby, doesn't win the race. How do you beat up, judge, berate your body? What would forgiveness look like?

FREE FALL: Sometimes spiritual study can feel very vulnerable, especially when our ideas about our self or reality are challenged. What might support you when you face this necessary vulnerability?

JOHN CAGE: John Cage (1912–1992) framed silence (environmental and unintended sounds) in his composition *4'33"*, creating a kind of artistic prayer from simple attention. Is all sound music? Does it depend on attention?

BURNOUT: The crises in our world are so many in number and so great in magnitude that those who give themselves to making things better often become burned out. What are a few simple, direct ways you can support someone with burnout, or before they hit that point? (Also try doing these for yourself!)

LESSONS FROM LEAVES: Ablaze with autumn color, leaves are brightest even as they face their final days. How might the fact of impermanence bring clarity and vitality to your meditation and daily life?

....
....
....
....
....
....
....

TRUST IN A DEWDROP: Master Dogen wrote, "The moon is in a dewdrop," pointing to how enlightenment (the moon) is reflected in even the smallest of things. Is there a small gesture you can make today to express your oneness with others?

....
....
....
....
....
....
....

ADULT IN THE ROOM: Have you ever been called to be the adult in the room while workmates were being self-centered? How was that for you?

....
....
....

....

....

....

....

....

....

A GOOD CRY: Reflect on a time when what your body seemed to need was a good, thoroughgoing cry. Did you allow this? Meditation halls where no one ever cries are like pots with their lids on too tight, always about to boil over; in healthy ones, tears come and go as part of cooking our lives with kindness and attention.

....

....

....

....

....

....

....

....

SUBTLETY: There's a difference between the breeze and the ancient, tender wind. Where do you find subtle shades of particularity that enrich your mind?

....

....

....

....

....

....

....

....

BECOMING FABULOUS: People can become overly precious about Zen art, and that earnestness can get in the way. Write an unexpected sentence here. Have some fun with it, let it be fabulous, let yourself go!

BEING UNPREDICTABLE: Oft-quoted Einstein: "We can't solve problems by using the same kind of thinking we used when we created them." What world problems might need a new kind of thinking?

WINTER

Some would say Zen is about what happens when we stop adding on, decorating, dragging along our baggage moment by moment—when we've let all that go cold. The night moon is in the treetops, there is no one looking for anything better. The wind is just the wind. The clock is not ticking. But when we describe the shadowed snow, our persistent patterns of seeing become evident. No matter how much baggage one sets down, we'll have patterns that persist. We will see based on what we saw before, we will still know something, even if it is that we do not know. And as that knowing intercedes, knower and known are separate, and the dualities align in their familiar places.

Winter, then, engenders a natural inquiry: Is it possible to have an intimate and authentic life? Whatever we do is inadequate, and doing nothing also falls short: this is the koan of being. How can we realize "snow hearing snow"— the language in which there is no stranger, no one apart from us? As you study winter with your pen, let it bring you home to an honorable and honest way of life.

BARE BRANCHES: The branches are bare; the heart's winter has arrived. In your meditation, let whatever you've been carrying rest in the snow of stillness. Reflect.

....
....
....
....
....
....
....

SNOW IN A SILVER BOWL: Snow in a silver bowl is hard to see: it is white on white. In Zen, this is a way of referring to something extra, carried around but not needed. Any snow in your bowl?

....
....
....
....
....
....
....

JUST THIS: The true nature of reality is ineffable, beyond description and conceptualization. Zen may use the word "suchness" for this, which is deliberately vague, yet on point. Does your work and life express suchness? If so, how so?

....
....
....

....

....

....

....

....

....

BUSY BODY: Give special attention today to the transition between your seated meditation and standing upright. Was your mind busy or quiet?

....

....

....

....

....

....

....

....

....

....

KNOW YOUR RACISM AND SEXISM: Many of us feel we would never be intentionally racist or sexist, yet we have patterns and presumptions that express prejudice, stereotyping, or discrimination. How have you worked to deepen your awareness around this?

....

....

....

....

....

....

....

....

TURN INWARD: Draw a line representing yourself turning inward.

GOOD PEOPLE: What are humanity's best qualities? Which of them do you find in yourself? (Any you might need to develop a bit?)

IN GRIEF: Winter is a time when the passing nature of all things becomes even more evident. Green life goes dormant, white blankets the ground. Write a few words, being gentle with yourself, about how grief informs your meditation.

WORDLESS: Sometimes words fail to express what our life is proving to be true. By definition, you can't write what is wordless, but can you identify times when this has been your experience?

SAVING ALL SENTIENT BEINGS: All beings suffer as part of being alive. Does your work, directly or indirectly, serve to reduce suffering? Are there categories of beings whose suffering particularly moves you (the elderly, the poor, endangered species, others)?

SHOWING UP: When we are genuinely called to show up for one another, there is an energy that supports us. Have others ever surprised you by showing up when you needed them? Have you ever been called to speak for the voiceless?

IRON GRINDSTONE LIU: "The Grindstone," Liu Tiemo (780–859), had a deep and playful relationship with her teacher. She is said to have fully realized the "undivided heart of being," and would go on to "grind away" at the half-baked understanding of her own students, helping them become free. Is there a "grindstone" who helps you let go?

BE NEW: What gesture might best indicate that you are open to something new? Describe or draw that gesture, and don't be afraid to amuse yourself in the process.

SNOW DIAMONDS: Describe a moment when the shine and sparkle that is light meeting snow stopped you in your tracks. (If you don't live where there's snow, has light on water ever taken your breath away?)

THE LONG SIT: There comes a day when instead of getting up from meditation after 10 minutes, it feels right to sit longer and go deeper. Some students will go on retreats where they sit for days in a row. Have you ever found longer periods of meditation helpful? How so?

....

....

....

....

....

....

....

VOWS: In Buddhism, a "bodhisattva" is someone so compassionate that they won't rest until everyone is free from needless suffering. To make a "bodhisattva vow" is to acknowledge that your personal peace requires that all beings find peace. How would a vow like that change your life?

....

....

....

....

....

....

TRUST YOURSELF: How might your work change if you trusted yourself more deeply? (Not that you'd be insulated from improvement, just confident enough not to hedge your bets.)

....

....

....

....
....
....
....
....

THE ACUPUNCTURE NEEDLE OF ZAZEN: Master Dogen wrote about Zen meditation, calling it "the acupuncture needle of zazen" because it addressed existential suffering. Write a few lines about your physical posture for meditation.

....
....
....
....
....
....
....
....
....

TO READ, OR NOT TO READ: Is reading the core texts and teachings in Buddhism helpful? If so, why? If not, why not?

....
....
....
....
....
....
....

SNOW: Paint a disappearing scene here using melting snow or rain (or tap water) as ink.

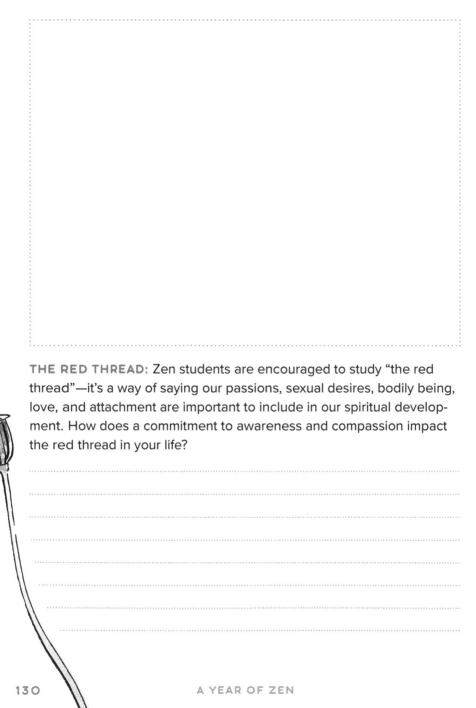

THE RED THREAD: Zen students are encouraged to study "the red thread"—it's a way of saying our passions, sexual desires, bodily being, love, and attachment are important to include in our spiritual development. How does a commitment to awareness and compassion impact the red thread in your life?

CURIOUSER AND CURIOUSER: What if you could become more curious and impartial toward your thoughts instead of being so easily persuaded by them? Write a few lines as you consider.

HOME MONASTERY: Traditional Zen practice arose from a monastic tradition that marked the group's activities throughout the day with ritual and ceremony. Today, these rituals are often adapted to help deepen mindful awareness at home. Sometimes ritual becomes rote, and not helpful. What makes the difference?

THE VERY HARD TALK TO GIVE: Sometimes, in all humility, it is our turn to lead. Have you found it easy to give talks, to teach and lead, or very hard?

....
....
....
....
....

MELTING ICE: Winter in cold climates arrives at a day when everything begins to melt. Find a frozen area, somewhere in your body where tension is being held, and spend a few minutes imagining it melting, with life flowing through it. How was that?

....
....
....
....
....
....
....

LEAVING A TEACHER: Graceful departures are too few. Reflect a bit on a time when you knew it was the right thing to leave either a teacher or other beloved. What did you learn?

....
....
....
....
....
....
....
....

SNOW TRACKS: Paint or draw what animal the tracks in the snow belong to. (Every moment has the "track" of what came before. In this case, let it be an animal, and get to know it.)

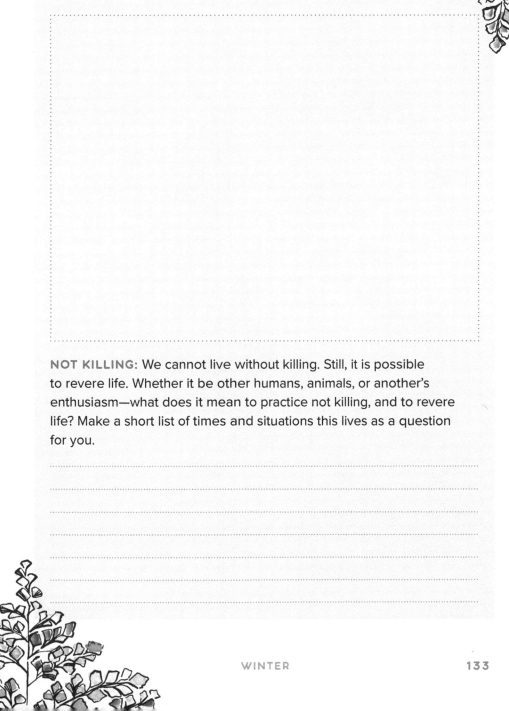

NOT KILLING: We cannot live without killing. Still, it is possible to revere life. Whether it be other humans, animals, or another's enthusiasm—what does it mean to practice not killing, and to revere life? Make a short list of times and situations this lives as a question for you.

BLUE SKY MIND: If we believe in our thoughts as reliable accounts of reality, sometimes we'll find they become something of a weather system—which we then live in for days, years, even decades. And, suddenly, the sky clears. Have you ever had a shift or breakthrough like this?

....

....

....

....

....

....

....

NOW HIT THE BELL: To taste the mind in its most relaxed, open, poised state, here's an exercise. Find a small bell, and ring it every 10 seconds or so for several minutes. Put your attention on the space between the hits, the silence that makes the sound evident. Reflect.

....

....

....

....

....

....

FOLLOW THE MONEY: Are you at peace around money's place in your life? What are, or have been, some of the struggles?

....

....

....

....
....
....
....

FULL ENERGY: Zen is a mountain climb, out of the valley of yearning and loss, to the vista where we see the wholeness of the terrain. Still, it is just one step after another. Have you ever put yourself so into your practice that your effort disappears?

....
....
....
....
....
....
....

THE OCEANIC STOREHOUSE: There are "108 billion" (in other words, uncountable) letters in the teachings of Buddhism. To study this ocean-large canon means the student's life is realized as immeasurable as well. Is this daunting? Comforting?

....
....
....
....
....
....
....

TAMING THE OX: The ox runs wild in the field; the ox is you, and the field is this whole, great earth. Write a few lines about how wildness and taming exist for you. Are there negative consequences to wildness? Is it possible to tame the mind? Is it important?

TRUE NATURE: American Buddhist and activist Joanna Macy said, "Our true nature is to be part of one another." We need to understand that nature, rather than a reserve of materials passively awaiting our use, is alive. Reflect on the pleasures and responsibilities of true nature—humanity's, and great earth's as well.

DON'T GO TO WAR: The individual sense of self is relative, not all that we are; still, without it, we'd be unable to cross the street without being hit by a car. Yet often as we meditate, rather than simply forget the self, we kind of declare war on it. How can you stop the war without getting caught up in yourself?

WINTER FLOWER VASE: At the monastery one winter morning, it was so cold in the meditation hall the flower vase on the altar cracked as ice formed. Though not about creating discomfort, sometimes spiritual life is just not comfortable. How do you appreciate this?

LEGACY: When you meditate, the wisdom and commitment of all those who've meditated before you is present. You carry their legacy, and add to the legacy of sincerity and compassion flowing forward in time. When you think of your work, whose legacy do you carry, and how do you keep it flowing forward?

NOT TOO MUCH, NOT TOO LITTLE: In Zen, drugs and alcohol are to be used in moderation or not at all. And keen awareness is given to not "selling substances," meaning weakening anyone else's clarity. Is there anything you need to bring into balance in this area?

ARRIVING AT WINTER: Winter is sometimes used in Zen teachings to indicate the absolute, where nothing can be differentiated from anything else in an ultimate, permanent sense. Given that, can anyone arrive at winter? (Don't get in a language-knot, just write from your heart!)

ORIGINAL FACE: You may have a transforming glimpse beyond the confines of the usual sense of self. Zen might call this seeing your "original face." Still, the relative self does not disappear. Make a quick and playful drawing of this original face.

NETWORKING: Everything arises and is conditioned by everything else: it's a vast, amazing network of relations. Make a quick list of five people, places, or things that have influenced you positively.

BOREDOM: Boredom happens. Your meditation, on one day or many, may feel like watching paint dry. How might you encourage someone new to practice when boredom is making it hard for them to remember this will change?

INSIDE OUT: Use the cosmic mudra to give you feedback. During meditation rest your hands in your lap palms up, knuckles overlapping, thumbs touching gently. Do your thumbs drift when your mind does? How else does outside reflect inside in your body?

TIP BIG: Acknowledge others' work today. If you can, leave an outrageous tip. Whose work has made your life easier this week?

....

....

....

....

MEN IN POWER: Community is regarded as one of the great treasures in Buddhism and a profound support for individual practice. Men in power have sometimes made communal groups a dangerous place for women (and other men) to practice, using hierarchy to take sexual advantage of openheartedness. What can be done? What are you called to do?

....

....

....

....

....

....

....

....

....

....

FOOTPRINTS OF THE ANCESTORS: What spiritual figure in history would you like to have a chance to talk with in depth?

....

....

....

....

....

....

....

....

PAINTING WINTER: How does winter enter a painting? Draw winter in the space below.

SOLACE: The Buddha, after years of searching out spiritual teachings from others, returned home and sat alone under a tree he remembered offering solace in his childhood. What place do you return to that brings peace to your mind? Describe with details.

GRANDIOSITY: We can get kind of puffed up with the grandness of seeking enlightenment. We take the noble posture of the Buddha when we sit, and can think that means we're somehow special. Have you ever noticed this "puffed-upped-ness" in yourself, or perhaps easier, in someone else?

....

....

....

....

....

....

....

....

YOU WILL NOT BE FORGOTTEN: Consider someone who has died alone or left behind no loving relatives or friends. Write "You will not be forgotten" several times below. Even without knowing a name, this matters.

....

....

....

....

....

....

....

ALONE BETWEEN HEAVEN AND EARTH: Integrity can always be deepened. Consider your work for a few minutes: Is there any part of it where you sometimes overtly or subtly slip out of integrity? Privately and gently acknowledge those places.

....

....

RETURN TO THE BASICS: A meditative life takes place in the body. Are you honoring the temple that you are by getting the best sleep you can, eating well, keeping it moving, etc.?

HOST AND GUEST: Sometimes, we know how to answer (be the host), but we forget how to ask (be the guest). "Host and guest" is used in Zen, like everything else, to clarify who we really are. How about you— are you equally at ease whether host or guest?

INTIMACY: Have you ever experienced being so intimate with something that "it" no longer feels apart from "you"? At that moment, the reference system we usually use to analyze, judge, understand, and know is gone. This is the intimacy of "When you walk, just walk. When you cry, just cry." Reflect.

DO WHAT YOU'RE DOING: It sounds so simple, "Do what you're doing while you're doing it." What gets in the way?

THE BACKWARD STEP: Meditation is called "taking the backward step and turning the light inward." Sometimes we get a little scared of what we might see or what will happen if we're not pushing forward. What does not getting or going anywhere bring up for you?

....

....

....

....

....

....

....

NO ONE IS A STORY: Pick someone familiar and try to see them without whatever story you have about them. Let them be new. Really see, hear, feel them. What hadn't you noticed before?

....

....

....

....

....

....

....

....

I'VE GOT YOU COVERED: There is tremendous vulnerability just under the surface of much of our life at work. How can you, without being obvious, back up a colleague to make them feel safe and appreciated?

....

....

....

....

....

....

....

....

LEAVE A LITTLE: There's a value in cleaning your plate. But today, leave a small portion of each meal uneaten, so that the decision to end the meal is your own, not the plate's. Reflect.

....

....

....

....

....

....

....

....

....

MOUNTAINS ARE MOUNTAINS: Master Dogen said, "When we devote ourselves to studying the sutras, they truly come forth. These sutras are the mountains, rivers, great earth, plants and trees." Has "the great earth" ever struck you as a holy teaching (sutra)?

....

....

....

....

....

....

....

....

WILLOW ARE GREEN: Zen practice helps us quit the habit of living in abstraction and return to the wholeness of reality and the particularity of each thing. List five "particulars" in the room right now.

....

....

....

....

....

....

....

....

....

INDOOR CATS: Cats raised indoors don't learn to look up, and are easy prey for hunting birds. We all wear blinders of some sort. Have you noticed any pattern to your own not-noticing?

....

....

....

....

....

....

....

....

....

....

....

BELLS AND WHISTLES: As you get started with a meditation practice, don't add too many bells and whistles or make it an excuse to shop for spiritual stuff. Have you begun accumulating Zen things (or ideas)?

NO EXPLANATION: All of Zen's rituals are pointing to one thing: the reality of no separation between the self and the "ten thousand things" (the whole universe). Like a caress, a bow can't really be explained, just experienced. Reflect.

NO MATTER HOW HARD YOU TRY: Sometimes, we do our best, try our hardest, and we still can't get the job done. It's hard to trust that succeed or fail, the process is also what it's about. When have you experienced trusting the process?

YOU ARE STILL THAT KIDDO: Adults can get in a rut, where the only utter release and pleasure takes place in very narrow channels (sexually, for instance). Think back to your childhood; what did you completely enjoy?

MOUNTAINS ARE NO LONGER MOUNTAINS: A photographer wants to take a picture of a mountain. He diligently hikes uphill with his camera, and later realizes his pictures just look like trail and woods, not "mountain." When we stop separating ourselves—from a person, a place, a thing—they are no longer out there, other, and our names and stories about them stop functioning. When has a mountain stopped being a mountain in your life?

THE GREAT WAY HAS NO GATE: You can't enter Zen because there is no place it isn't. Still, we practice. In a sense, Zen's completeness actually depends on our practice. Try writing a few lines about how life depends on you showing up.

MOTHER TURTLE: The mother turtle comes ashore, lays her eggs, and returns to sea, covering her tracks in the sand by brushing her tail left to right. Of course, she has then left a trail of tail marks. One thing always leads to, or conditions, another. How does this play out politically?

COMFORT AND COMFORTING: As you inhale, breathe in the troubles of everyone you love; as you exhale, send healing and comfort. Do you notice that after several breaths, you have also comforted your own heart-mind?

....

....

....

....

....

....

....

....

NEVER FAR: Call to mind someone you have loved who died. Is there some object you could hold nearby for a while to help remember them and keep them feeling close?

....

....

....

....

....

....

....

SECRET GIFTS: Everyone has certain superpowers, whether it's making the world's best coffee, having a talent for perseverance, or being able to bring a smile or a song. What are the superpowers of several people you work with? How about yourself?

....

....

....

....
....
....
....
....

WALK IN THE GRAVEYARD: What is your preference for what is done with your body after you die? Cremation? Embalm and bury? Donate to science? Other?

....
....
....
....
....
....
....
....

MOUNTAINS ARE MOUNTAINS AGAIN: People are distinct, and the differences make all the difference! We can all be one and still get on each other's nerves. Reflect on a time when the seeming chasm between you and someone else became lucidly clear, and either bugged you or refreshed you.

....
....
....
....
....
....
....

BURN THE BUDDHA IMAGE: Have you ever had your image of what holy (or sacred or good) looks like get in the way of really seeing how it is present? Write a bit about getting over these images and ideas.

_____

_____

_____

_____

_____

_____

_____

_____

_____

GREED CREEPS IN: Whether it is for material things or spiritual accomplishments, we're always dealing with greed. We want more, even as we forget to taste the food on our plate. Where do you find yourself getting a little greedy?

_____

_____

_____

_____

_____

_____

_____

_____

_____

_____

_____

INSIDE JOB: Wrap yourself in a warm blanket or coat and meditate outside for five to ten minutes in the cold. See what thoughts come up, what sensations, where your mind wants to go. Keep returning to the "cozy space" of your own attention. Reflect.

MAKING VISIBLE THE INVISIBLE: Write an apology that you'd want to make if you had only one day to live. It is enough to simply write "I'm sorry."

NOT HOLDING ON: Instead of waiting until you die to give things away, what might you make a gift of before you go?

DON'T FUSS: What bothers you more: being fussed over when you're sick or not being cared for adequately?

PEBBLE HITTING BAMBOO: Sometimes we put in great effort to no effect. Other times some small, unexpected thing opens a gate that had been blocked. Does this make it harder for you to work hard? Or easier?

FORWARD AND BACKWARD: What was the earliest hard decision you had to make? What was the most recent? What do you see ahead that may require a difficult choice?

WHEN YOU LAUGH, JUST LAUGH: Life ties itself into seeming knots, and then suddenly releases. You can't figure it out, but you can enjoy the journey. When was the last time a belly laugh took you over?

YOUR WILDERNESS: The Buddha realized enlightenment when he saw the morning star appear in the sky. Write about the last time you let yourself be silent under a starry sky.

....

....

....

....

....

....

....

LIMINAL HEART: The waiting areas between one point in time and space and the next are liminal spaces. There, we feel a sense of being on the verge of something. Practice holding that liminal space in your heart, wordlessly. Now, say a word!

....

....

....

....

....

....

....

....

IT'S REALLY JUST LOVE: Work is just love made manifest. Life is just love made manifest. Are these statements true?

....

....

....

JUST BOW: Our ego will always want to assert itself: that's what it does. In a private space, practice letting yourself drop to the floor in a full bow. Don't bow "to" anything, just let your ego fall away for a few seconds and your body do the bowing. Reflect.

NOT THE TIME OF YIN AND YANG: All the ways we divide ourselves are illusion (oneness is also illusion!). To study these illusions, we sit, study, create, embody, serve. What can you do to realize this more deeply?

THE PAINTER IS THE BRUSH: Your life is your art. Draw a line that begins, continues, and ends with ki (sheer life force).

WHERE DOES IT END?: An epitaph is a statement that honors some-one who has died. Sometimes you see them on gravestones. In five to ten words, write an epitaph for the world as you've known it.

Finish each day and be done with it. You have done what you could. Some blunders and absurdities no doubt crept in; forget them as soon as you can. Tomorrow is a new day. You shall begin it serenely and with too high a spirit to be encumbered with your old nonsense.

–Ralph Waldo Emerson

PARTING WORDS

To have a daily writing practice is no small thing. To have given yourself to this year-long exploration of Zen means you no doubt faced what many will go to great lengths to avoid facing. Some days I'm sure the assignments were just plain irritating and you shouted at me through the ether, "What? What does this have to do with Zen?" Or, "I don't even know what you're asking!" Or, "You already asked that several weeks ago; why again?" If you're like most of us, there were days (weeks? months?) when you didn't even enter the "zendo," the place of practice . . . and then you found your way back. I hope there were also times when you were simply, fully, creatively engaged, loving what you encountered. All of this—the irritations and aggravations, the periods of avoidance or laziness, the returns to earnestness, the love and enthusiasm—is the stuff a full-out Zen practice comprises. "There's been a whole lot of reality going on," a student of mine used to explain when he'd come back after having disappeared from practice for a while. Indeed, and always. One of the sweetest gifts of Zen is that it always welcomes us back. As you discovered in this year of writing, each day is a new empty space. You breathe it to life. That's how it stays honest, not reliant on others or ideologies, but tender and true.

So, what happens when you've completed this sacred year of writing practice? One option (and one I'm sure my publisher would love) is that you buy another copy of this journal and begin a fresh year with it. The same assignments will garner quite different writing a second (or twentieth) time through. Another option is that you continue daily Zen writing practice without the external prompts. Just write. Trust your heart-mind to present what is relevant and genuinely calling you. If you notice you've gotten into a rut, shake it up, give yourself a different kind of language challenge, like the ways you've practiced this year.

For some of you, the writing will be a support in developing the seven areas (meditation, liturgy, work, art, study, body, world) as windows into seeing every aspect of your life as a place of practice. It can help to sit every day, have some rituals that remind you that this life is a gift and a sacred journey, and that your real work is much more than your job. Use study practice, art, and body practice to stimulate your physical, creative, and intellectual growth. And commit to the world, the seasons, the animals, the waters, and green life, as well as the political and cultural humanity we're creating together. If you'd like to study further with a Zen teacher and community: we are here for you. I am here for you. Just make your way to the door and knock.

RESOURCES

ON WRITING

Art & Fear: Observations on The Perils (and Rewards) of Artmaking
by David Bayles & Ted Orlando
> Originally published in 1994, *Art & Fear* is now an underground classic, full of relatable, valuable advice.

Bird by Bird by Anne Lamott
> Lamott shares herself and her craft, including anecdotes that tie the pieces together into all-around great writing.

The Elements of Style by William Strunk Jr. and E. B. White
> Strunk and White offer a guidebook of truths that support clear and beautiful writing.

Letters to a Young Poet by Rainer Maria Rilke
> Rilke's work is timeless and endlessly quotable.

On Writing Well by William Zinsser
> Considered a classic, Zinsser's book addresses nonfiction writers and includes writing tips, as well as the fundamentals of the craft.

The Paris Review Interviews
> In-depth interviews with some of the leading names in modern literature going back decades, including novelists, playwrights, and poets (Ernest Hemingway, T. S. Eliot, Kurt Vonnegut, Toni Morrison, among others).

The Writing Life by Annie Dillard
> Dillard discusses the challenges of writing and makes clear the imperative. Beautifully crafted.

Writing Down the Bones by Natalie Goldberg
> Goldberg explores writing as spiritual practice, the basics of honest writing, the importance of learning how to listen. Inspiring and generous and first among her tall pile of wonderful, helpful books. (Natalie also does online courses; check her website for details.)

The Writing Life: Writers on How They Think and Work
edited by Marie Arana
> Arana draws from a decade of *The Washington Post*'s "Writing Life" column, with contributors as diverse as Jimmy Carter, Joyce Carol Oates, and Carl Sagan.

ZEN TEACHERS

The Essential Teachings of Zen Master Hakuin
by Hakuin Ekaku, translated by Norman Waddell
> Hakuin (1685–1768) was one of Zen's great revitalizers, and is credited with revamping Japanese Zen after it had been in decline for over 300 years. Created the "What is the sound of one hand clapping?" koan and many others. Also a highly respected painter and calligrapher.

Moon in a Dewdrop: Teachings of Eihei Dogen
translated by Kazuaki Tanahashi
> Japanese Buddhist priest, writer, poet, philosopher, and founder of the Soto school of Zen in Japan, Dogen's teachings are profound, beautiful, and challenging.

Rengetsu: Life and Poetry of Lotus Moon translated by John Stevens
> Japanese nun whose life and art give tremendous lessons in resilience and generosity. Rengetsu's prodigious poetry, calligraphy, and pottery are highly regarded and much sought after.

The Zen of Creativity: Cultivating Your Artistic Life by John Daido Loori
> Loori powerfully explores the traditional Zen arts (calligraphy, poetry, painting, the tea ceremony, and flower arranging) as they meet modern art forms such as photography.

Zen Women: Beyond Tea Ladies, Iron Maidens, and Macho Masters
by Grace Schireson
> Of particular interest is the chapter titled "Iron Grindstone Liu."
> In this wonderful offering, Schireson gathers the accounts of many of Zen's female ancestors who had largely been left out of the official, male-devised records. Meet teachers from the time of the Buddha and continuing through from China, Korea, and Japan.

ACKNOWLEDGMENTS

My gratitude to the students who have studied Zen with me, and written with me in Zen Journal retreats and workshops. It has been a privilege beyond words. Thank you for inspiring this book.

The seven areas of practice used to shape this book will be familiar to those who train in the Mountains and Rivers Order as being similar to the Monastery's "eight gates." My gratitude to John Daido Loori for his many dedicated and creative years of teaching. During my early years at Zen Mountain Monastery, he tasked me with developing a curriculum for various areas of practice, creating an outline of study that would extend over 10 distinct stages and many years of training. The program would evolve over decades; I have no doubt its shortcomings were mine and its greatest strengths were due to Roshi's continuing vision.

Deep appreciation also to having had the chance to study and teach with Peter Matthiessen, Allen Ginsberg, and Natalie Goldberg. Each modeled writing as a Way, and directly encouraged me to consider pen and paper as my zendo.

ABOUT THE AUTHOR

 **BONNIE MYOTAI TREACE, SENSEI,** is the founder of Hermitage Heart Zen. She lives in Black Mountain, North Carolina. Sensei was the first successor in the Mountains and Rivers Order, and is a Zen priest and teacher. She led Zen training in the Catskills and in New York City for several decades. For many years, her *Zen Journal* and *Writers Island* attracted many hundreds of students to explore the relationship between writing and Zen practice. She hosted and taught with Allen Ginsberg, Peter Matthiessen, Natalie Goldberg, and many other writers and artists as part of a celebrated curriculum on the Zen Arts. In North Carolina, she offers writing retreats as well as at-home meditation and stress reduction instruction to those who cannot attend retreats due to disability or old age.

Sensei is the author of four books: *Winter Moon*, *Empty Branches*, *Wake Up*, and *Zen Meditation for Beginners*. She is married, is the adopted grandmother of two amazing grandkids, and lives with a long-haired cat and gigantic collie.